# BREAKFAST IN BED

# Breakfast in Bed

## Morning Menus
## for Sensational Beginnings

## by Connie McCole

### Illustrations by Cynthia Fitting

HEARST BOOKS
NEW YORK

Library of Congress Cataloging-in-Publication Data

McCole, Connie
Breakfast in bed : morning menus for sensational beginnings / by
Connie McCole ; illustrations by Cynthia Fitting.
        p.        cm.
ISBN 0-688-10724-9
1. Breakfasts.  2. Menus.  I. Title.
        TX733.M47    1992
641.5'2—dc20                        91-15879
                                    CIP

Printed in Singapore

First Edition

1   2   3   4   5   6   7   8   9   10

*For Jim, who
makes breakfast
in bed special*

ACKNOWLEDGMENTS

I would like to thank Rita Aero
and Esther Mitgang of Fly
Productions for their generous
assistance and patience, and for
having confidence in me.

   Thanks also to my friend,
Cynthia Coleman, for bringing
me together with Fly Productions.

   To my dear husband, Jim,
and my two fabulous sons,
Christopher and Ryan, thanks for
your enthusiasm and for being
my best critics.

# CONTENTS

# INTRODUCTION

What is it that is so delightful about that unique ritual called "breakfast in bed"? The very thought of it makes us slow down and fantasize. Bed, that warm, soothing retreat where spirits are nourished and dreams are made. Breakfast, a meal with limitless possibilities that we seldom take the time to truly enjoy.

I have created ten breakfast menus that will transport you to fabulous locations around the world — from Scotland to Santa Fe, from Morocco to Manhattan. I had a wonderful time developing the menus and recipes that accompany them, and I know you will enjoy preparing and serving them. *Breakfast in Bed* may offer only a small break from reality, but please don't underestimate the rejuvenating power of a delicious morning adventure for two.

Because your escape will be more relaxing if you have done some advance planning, each breakfast menu has a section called "The Night Before." This describes preparations that may be done in advance to minimize cooking time in the morning and get you out of the kitchen and back into bed as quickly as possible. I have estimated preparation times for both "The Night Before" and your "Wake Up Call" the next morning. All recipes serve two of course.

Along with each breakfast you will find serving suggestions to help you set the stage for your morning adventure. So dust off those rarely used treasures you've hidden away and create a summer Morning in Provence or an elegant Venice Awakening. Maybe you're in the mood for a healthy California Spa Starter or for the exotic First Light in Bangkok. Whatever your fantasy — you're in for a daybreak adventure that is easy, entertaining, and absolutely delicious.

7

# Morning in Provence

*Iced Flute of Champagne*

*French Toast Avignon*

*Warm Peppered Ham*

*Sun-Ripened Figs with Lavender Honey*

The unforgettable romance of an early morning in the south of France is captured in this elegant breakfast. The sweet French toast and honey drizzled figs are deliciously complemented by the peppery ham. Pop the cork on a bottle of your favorite Champagne and *Voilà! Petit dejeuner au lit!*

PREPARATION TIMES
*The Night Before — Fifteen Minutes*
*Wake Up Call — Twenty Minutes*

## THE NIGHT BEFORE

*For the Champagne:*  Put the Champagne and glasses in the refrigerator to chill.

*For the French Toast:*  Combine all of the ingredients except the bread in a shallow dish. Put the bread slices into the mixture, turning them and gently poking them with a fork so they absorb the mixture. Cover the baking dish with plastic wrap and refrigerate, turning the bread over once before you go to bed.

*For the Peppered Ham:*  If your butcher carries pepper-coated ham, purchase one-quarter pound sliced about one-quarter inch thick. Or, you can pepper your own ham by placing two thick slices of ham or Canadian bacon sprinkled with coarsely ground black pepper between two pieces of plastic wrap and gently pounding, using a meat pounder or your fist. Wrap and refrigerate.

*Prepare the Breakfast Trays:*  Line white wicker trays with bright cotton print fabric or place mats, or line any other trays with woven mats. Napkins of contrasting color would complement the bright cotton print, while delicate floral napkins would be *comme il faut* with the woven mat. Roll the napkins up and tie them with ribbons.

## ICED FLUTE OF CHAMPAGNE

The bubbles will be delightfully effervescent and last longer if the Champagne is served in tall, thin glasses known as flutes. You will also want an ice bucket nearby to keep the bottle properly chilled. Sipping Champagne is a lovely way to pass the moments while the French toast is cooking. Place a fresh raspberry or two in each flute for a Provençal aperitif.

## FRENCH TOAST AVIGNON

2 large eggs plus 2 egg whites
2 tablespoons Grand Marnier
1 tablespoon sugar
1/8 teaspoon salt
3 tablespoons milk
1/8 teaspoon vanilla extract
Grated zest of 1/2 large orange
Juice of 1 large orange
4 slices French or sourdough bread, cut 3/4 inch thick
Butter for frying

Remove the bread from the refrigerator. Melt about one teaspoon of butter in a skillet over medium-low heat. Fry the bread for five to six minutes on each side, or until golden brown. Divide between two warm dinner plates and set aside.

## WARM PEPPERED HAM

Remove the peppered ham from the refrigerator. When the French toast is done, cook the ham over medium-high heat in the same pan. Do not clean the pan. Fry the ham for two minutes on each side. The sugar used to cure the ham will give it a caramel color when it is cooked. Place the ham next to the French toast on the dinner plate.

## SUN-RIPENED FIGS WITH LAVENDER HONEY

Select six large or ten small ripe figs. They should "give" a bit when lightly pressed between your thumb and forefinger. Cut each fig lengthwise into quarters, but leave them joined at the bottom so they will open into "flowers." Arrange them on two dessert plates and drizzle about a teaspoon of lavender honey over the figs; be a bit more generous if the figs do not have enough natural sugar for your taste.

## SERVING BREAKFAST IN PROVENCE

Slip a sprig or two of fresh lavender, jasmine, or rosemary in each napkin. Arrange the dinner plates of French toast and ham, and the dessert plates of honeyed figs on the trays. Add a Provençal touch to your bedroom with a bouquet of sunflowers in a pottery pitcher. Now, jump back into bed and offer the toast "*Salut!*"

# SANTA FE SUNRISE

*Tequila Sunrise*

*Chili Relleno Soufflé*

*Whole-Wheat Tortillas with Avocado Pesto*

*Iced Watermelon Slices with Lime*

The Santa Fe Sunrise is a color-splashed and festive breakfast adventure. The chilies and tequila will warm you through, while the avocado and watermelon cool the palate. This spirited Southwest-style morning is a great way to launch a special day — any time of the year.

PREPARATION TIMES
*The Night Before — Twenty Minutes*
*Wake Up Call — Thirty Minutes*

## THE NIGHT BEFORE

*For the Chili Relleno Soufflé:* Lightly butter two individual baking dishes. Slip a strip of cheese into each chili and divide the stuffed chilies equally between the baking dishes. Cover and refrigerate.

Combine the flour, salt, and nutmeg in a blender or food processor. Process to blend and let sit, covered, overnight.

Dice the tomato. Wash and separate the cilantro. Wrap and refrigerate.

*Prepare the Breakfast Trays:* Decorate each breakfast tray with a boldly striped place mat (use fabric, towels, gift wrap, construction paper, or small serapes). Add a tiny potted cactus to each tray.

## TEQUILA SUNRISE

Pour one-half ounce grenadine into each of two tall glasses. Add ice. Pour one ounce tequila (optional) and then one-quarter cup freshly squeezed orange juice over the ice in each glass. Stir once, gently, to create a colorful "sunrise" effect.

## CHILI RELLENO SOUFFLÉ

3 ounces Monterey Jack or Havarti cheese, cut into 1/2- by 3-inch strips
One 4-ounce can whole fire-roasted green chilies, drained
1/4 cup all-purpose flour
Scant 1/4 teaspoon salt
Dash of nutmeg
1 tomato, peeled, seeded, and diced, for garnish
Sprigs of fresh cilantro for garnish
2 large eggs, separated, plus 1 egg white
1 cup milk

Preheat the oven to 350°F. Separate the eggs. Put the three egg whites in a large mixing bowl and set aside. Add the egg yolks and milk to the dry mixture in the blender or food processor. Process until the mixture is smooth.

Beat the egg whites until they hold firm peaks. Gently fold the yolk mixture into the whites, until no traces of white remain. Spoon the mixture evenly over the chilies in their individual baking dishes, and bake for 12 to 15 minutes, or until a toothpick inserted into the center of the egg mixture comes out clean. Remove the dishes from the oven and sprinkle diced tomato down the center of each soufflé. Scatter sprigs of fresh cilantro over the top.

### WHOLE-WHEAT TORTILLAS WITH AVOCADO PESTO

Warm four foil-wrapped whole-wheat tortillas in the oven for five minutes. Peel, pit, and coarsely mash one ripe avocado. Squeeze a small clove of garlic through a garlic press and stir it into the avocado. Add a pinch of salt and lime juice to taste. Spread the Avocado Pesto on the warm tortillas and roll them into cylinders.

### ICED WATERMELON SLICES WITH LIME

Arrange two thick half-moon slices of ice-cold watermelon on chilled dessert plates. Cut one lime into quarters. Squeeze one-quarter lime over each slice of watermelon and discard the skins. Place the remaining lime quarters on top of the watermelon slices.

### SERVING BREAKFAST IN SANTA FE

Arrange two rolled tortillas each and a fresh-from-the-oven soufflé on two large colorful plates. Surround with the chilled dishes of watermelon and the Tequila Sunrises. Orchestrate your Southwestern breakfast adventure with acoustic guitar, countrywestern, or mariachi music. *¡Olé!*

# VENICE AWAKENING

*Bridge of Sighs Bellini*

*Baked Peaches "La Serenissima"*

*Polenta with Prosciutto and Mascarpone*

*Espresso con Limone*

Breakfast *con brio* opens with the celebrated aperitif of Venice,
the Bellini, a delicate combination of fresh peaches and
sparkling wine. Steaming-hot bowls of polenta, warm peaches
filled with crisp amaretti crumbs, and cups of invigorating
espresso enhance the magic mood that is Venice.

PREPARATION TIMES
*The Night Before — Five Minutes*
*Wake Up Call — Thirty Minutes*

## The Night Before

*For the Baked Peaches:* Use a rolling pin to crush two packages (each one contains two cookies) of amaretti still in their wrappers into coarse chunks. Tighten the wrappers on each one by twisting the ends, or if torn, replace with plastic wrap and set aside.

*Prepare the Breakfast Trays:* Cover two trays with red-checked cloths. Add matching napkins and Italian pottery. On each tray, place a tiny glass carafe filled with sprigs of sweet basil to scent the room.

## Bridge of Sighs Bellini

Peel one ripe peach: Submerge it in boiling water for ten seconds, rinse in cold water, and remove the skin. Cut the peach in half, remove the stone, and purée the fruit in the blender with one-quarter teaspoon lemon juice. Place two tablespoons purée in each stemmed glass and fill the glasses with Prosecco (sparkling white wine of the region) or Champagne. Stir and serve immediately. Enjoy the Bellinis while the peaches and polenta are cooking.

## Baked Peaches "La Serenissima"

Preheat the oven to 375°F. Cut one large ripe peach in half and remove the stone. Do not peel. Enlarge the stone cavity by cutting out and discarding about a tablespoon of peach flesh from each half. Divide the peach halves

between two lightly buttered individual baking dishes. Empty one packet of crushed amaretti into each of the peach hollows. Dot each with butter and sprinkle with one-half teaspoon sugar. Bake the peaches for fifteen minutes. Sprinkle with a few drops rum, brandy, or Amaretto, and bake for ten minutes more, or until the peaches are tender.

## POLENTA WITH PROSCIUTTO AND MASCARPONE

1 1/2 cups chicken stock
3/4 cup polenta (coarse-ground yellow cornmeal)
1 1/2 cups milk
2 1/2 ounces prosciutto, sliced medium thick and cut into 1/2-inch
squares
1/2 cup mascarpone (if mascarpone is not available, substitute a semi-
soft, mild cheese such as Bel Paese or fresh mozzarella, grated)

Bring the chicken stock to a boil in a medium saucepan. Reduce the heat to medium low. Very gradually pour in the polenta, stirring constantly so it does not become lumpy. Add the milk one-quarter cup at a time, stirring constantly, and cook, stirring for eight minutes, or until thick like oatmeal and soft in texture. Stir in the prosciutto and all but two tablespoons of the cheese. Stir the polenta, remove from the heat, and spoon into heated serving bowls. Garnish with the remaining cheese.

### Espresso con Limone

Just before you are ready to eat, prepare the espresso and pour into demi-tasse or espresso cups. Slice two slivers of zest from a lemon and place one on each saucer together with one or two sugar cubes.

### Serving Breakfast in Venice

Place the bowls of polenta on large plates and accompany them with crusty Italian rolls for a delicious contrast in textures. Arrange the baked peaches on the trays along with the small cups of espresso. Now, throw open the windows and play a stirring aria from your favorite opera for this unique Venetian morning.

# Daybreak in Scotland

*Highland Four-Grain Griddle Cakes*

*Bonny Broiled Breakfast Sausage*

*Sautéed Cinnamon Pears with Candied Ginger*

*Isle of Skye Hot Chocolate*

On a bonny, brisk morning, curl up under the covers with a heartwarming Highlands breakfast. Stacks of four-grain griddle cakes, sizzling breakfast sausages, and sautéed pears crisp with ginger are a glorious way to stay warm inside and out. You may be tempted to stay in bed all day.

PREPARATION TIMES
*The Night Before — Thirty Minutes*
*Wake Up Call — Twenty-Five Minutes*

# THE NIGHT BEFORE

*For the Highland Griddle Cakes:* Put the oatmeal in the bowl of a food processor fitted with the steel blade and grind to a powder. Add the flours, cornmeal, baking powder, baking soda, and salt and process to combine. Let this mixture sit overnight in the covered food processor bowl.

*For the Breakfast Sausage:* Place four uncooked breakfast link sausages in a small sauté pan. Sprinkle them with one-half teaspoon rubbed sage and add just enough water to cover the sausages. Bring the water to a boil, reduce the heat, and let the sausages simmer gently for twenty minutes. Remove and drain. Let the sausages cool for a few minutes before wrapping and refrigerating them.

*For the Sautéed Pears:* Finely mince two teaspoons candied ginger. Wrap and set aside at room temperature.

*For the Hot Chocolate:* Finely chop two ounces semisweet chocolate. Put the chocolate in a small bowl and add two and one-half tablespoons firmly packed brown sugar. Cover and set aside.

*Prepare the Breakfast Trays:* Line two breakfast trays with place mats in a lively tartan. Select napkins in a complementary solid color.

## HIGHLAND FOUR-GRAIN GRIDDLE CAKES

3 tablespoons quick-cooking oatmeal (not instant)
1/3 cup whole-wheat flour
3 tablespoons all-purpose flour
3 tablespoons yellow cornmeal
1 teaspoon baking powder
1/2 teaspoon baking soda
Scant 1/4 teaspoon salt
1 tablespoon unsalted butter, cold
1/2 cup buttermilk, plus up to 2 tablespoons additional
1 large egg
1 tablespoon maple syrup
Vegetable oil for frying

Cut the butter into small pieces. Add the butter to the dry ingredients in the food processor bowl and pulse until coarsely mixed. Combine the one-half cup buttermilk, the egg, and maple syrup in a measuring cup and stir. Add the mixture to the food processor and process until smooth. Let this batter sit for five to ten minutes while you begin preparing the sausages, pears, and hot chocolate.

Preheat a griddle or frying pan that has been lightly greased with vegetable oil. The batter should be only slightly thicker than heavy cream; if necessary, add an additional tablespoon or two of buttermilk. Pour about one-quarter cup batter for each cake (use a measuring cup) onto the griddle. Cook until the cakes are full of bubbles on top and lightly browned on the bottom, about two minutes. Turn with a spatula and brown the other sides.

Heat some maple syrup to accompany the griddle cakes.

## BONNY BROILED BREAKFAST SAUSAGE

Preheat the broiler. Place the parboiled sausages on the broiler pan about six inches away from the heat and cook them on all sides until browned on all sides, about 3 minutes, taking care not to burn them. Remove them from the broiler, cover, and keep warm until ready to serve.

## SAUTÉED CINNAMON PEARS WITH CANDIED GINGER

Peel and quarter one ripe pear and remove the core. Slice each quarter lengthwise into three slices. Melt one tablespoon butter in a nonstick pan. Add the pear slices and sprinkle them with the finely minced candied ginger. Cook the pears until soft but still a bit crisp, about one minute on each side. Sprinkle the pears with a very light dusting of cinnamon. Gently remove them from the pan with a spatula, set aside, and keep warm.

## ISLE OF SKYE HOT CHOCOLATE

Place the chopped chocolate and brown sugar in a medium saucepan and add two cups milk. Cook over medium heat, stirring with a wire whisk to completely dissolve the chocolate and sugar, until hot, steaming and frothy. Reduce the heat to very low to keep the hot chocolate warm.

## SERVING BREAKFAST IN SCOTLAND

Choose glazed stoneware dinner plates, and arrange a stack of griddle cakes and two sausages on each plate. Frame the griddle cakes with fans of the sautéed pear slices. Position the plates on the trays and add oversize mugs of steaming hot chocolate. On a table nearby, set a small pitcher filled with warmed maple syrup and another larger one filled with fresh or dried heather.

Cover your bed with wool lap blankets and drape one around your shoulders. Now, climb back into your warm and cozy bed and imagine yourself in an ancient Scottish castle — perched on the rugged cliffs, high above the chilly moors.

# Moscow Morning

*Georgian Potato Galette with Smoked Salmon*

*Sour Cherry Marbled Yogurt*

*Baltic-Style Black Tea*

*Toasted Siberian Rye*

Chase the chill of a wintry morning with a breakfast feast fit for a czarina. The crisp potato galette has an unexpected filling of smoked salmon. The marbled yogurt, sweet with vanilla and tangy with sour cherries, is an inspired version of this Georgian delicacy. A regal breakfast — Russian style.

PREPARATION TIMES
*The Night Before — Ten Minutes*
*Wake Up Call — Twenty-Five Minutes*

## THE NIGHT BEFORE

*Prepare the Sour Cherry Yogurt:*  Cover and store in the refrigerator.

*Prepare the Breakfast Trays:*  Evoke the elegance of old Saint Petersburg with a setting worthy of Catherine the Great. Line your trays with lace and set out your finest crystal and silver to create a Winter Palace mood. You may not need candlelight, but a glass votive candle on each tray will make your settings glow.

### GEORGIAN POTATO GALETTE WITH SMOKED SALMON

2 large baking potatoes, scrubbed (not more than 1 pound total)
2 to 3 tablespoons vegetable oil
Salt and freshly ground pepper to taste
3 ounces sliced smoked salmon, cut into 1/4-inch slivers
Sour cream for garnish

Using a knife, mandolin, or the thinnest blade of a food processor, slice the unpeeled potatoes about one-eighth inch thick.

Heat two tablespoons of oil in an eight-inch skillet or omelet pan over medium-high heat until very hot. Lower the heat to medium and arrange half of the potato slices in an overlapping pattern in the skillet. Sprinkle with salt and pepper. Reserve a few slivers of the smoked salmon for garnish and arrange the remaining slivers over the potatoes. Layer the remaining potatoes over the salmon, sprinkle with salt and pepper, and press

down on the potatoes with a wide spatula. Lower the heat slightly so that the potatoes brown but not burn. Cook for five to eight minutes, pressing down on the potatoes from time to time. When the galette is golden brown on the bottom, loosen it with a spatula and slide it out onto a large plate. If there is no oil left in the pan, add a little more and then flip the galette back into the pan, browned side up. Press down on the top and let it cook for five to eight minutes, or until the bottom is golden brown. The outside of the galette will be crisp, the interior slightly soft.

Before serving, cut the galette in half and top each half with a dollop of sour cream. Garnish the sour cream with the remaining slivers of smoked salmon. Chives are also a colorful addition. A tablespoon of caviar may replace the salmon garnish.

### SOUR CHERRY MARBLED YOGURT

Turn an eight-ounce container of vanilla yogurt into a bowl and stir until smooth. In a blender, purée one-half cup drained and pitted canned sour cherries. Spoon the puréed cherries onto the center of the yogurt, then zig-zag a knife through the yogurt in one direction and then the other. Do not overmix or you will spoil the marbled effect.

## BALTIC-STYLE BLACK TEA

For each cup of tea you will need one teaspoon black tea leaves and six ounces boiling water. Place the tea leaves in a warmed teapot, add the boiling water, and let the tea steep for five minutes. Pour the tea through a tea strainer into cups. Serve the tea with sugar and lemon slices. For real Russian-style tea, stir cherry jam into the tea in place of sugar.

## TOASTED SIBERIAN RYE

Just before you are ready to eat, cut two thick slices of fresh light rye bread and toast them to golden brown. Spread each slice with softened unsalted butter, and sprinkle the tops with a mixture of poppy seeds and toasted sesame seeds.

## SERVING BREAKFAST IN MOSCOW

Arrange one-half of the garnished potato galette and a slice of the Siberian rye toast on each dinner plate. Spoon the marbled yogurt into tall crystal goblets. Complete your Russian fantasy breakfast with cups of Baltic-style black tea while the melody of "Lara's Theme" from *Dr. Zhivago* plays softly in the background.

# CALIFORNIA SPA STARTER

*Big Sur Corn Crêpes*

*Mango-Mint Salsa*

*Three-Citrus Salad with Raspberry Purée*

*Spiced Chamomile Tea*

Set aside a relaxed morning to refresh your mind and renew your body with the California Spa Starter. The fluffy open-faced corn crêpes are complemented by the refreshing mango-mint salsa. The vibrant finish of the three-citrus salad is as stimulating visually as it is to the palate.

PREPARATION TIMES
*The Night Before — Twenty-Five Minutes*
*Wake Up Call — Twenty-Five Minutes*

# THE NIGHT BEFORE

*Prepare the Mango-Mint Salsa:* Cover and place in the refrigerator. Don't worry about the avocado discoloring — the lime juice will keep it bright and green.

*For the Three-Citrus Salad:* Peel the citrus fruit with a knife to remove the white pith and outer membrane. Section the fruit by holding each one over a bowl and slicing between the membranes, leaving the membranes intact for completely clean wedges of orange, grapefruit, and tangerine. Discard the membranes. Cover the bowl of fruit and refrigerate. Purée the raspberries in a blender until smooth. Place the sauce in a separate bowl, cover, and refrigerate.

*Prepare the Breakfast Trays:* Use pure white linen or white terry-cloth hand towels to line the serving trays. Roll up white napkins or terry facecloths and slip a pair of sunglasses into each roll just for fun. On each tray, float a large blossom — a magnolia, camellia, or gardenia — in a clear glass bowl of water.

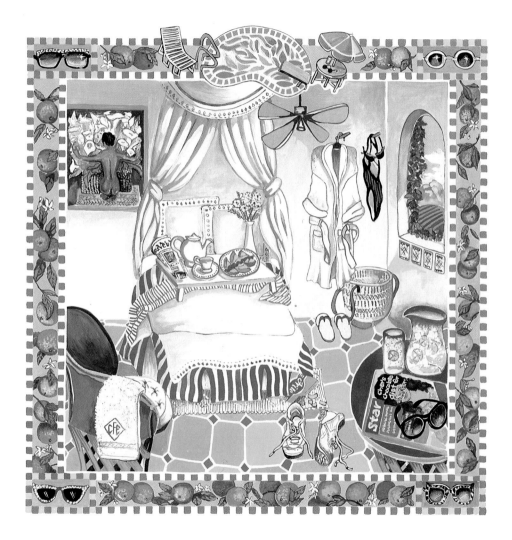

# Big Sur Corn Crêpes

1 large egg, separated, plus 1 egg white
1/2 cup frozen corn kernels, thawed
1/4 cup all-purpose flour
1/8 teaspoon salt
1/2 cup nonfat milk

Preheat the oven to 250°F.

Put the egg whites in a mixing bowl and set aside. Mix the egg yolk and corn kernels in a medium mixing bowl, using a fork. Stir in the flour and salt. Add the milk and stir until smooth.

Beat the egg whites until stiff but not dry. Fold the beaten egg whites into the corn batter.

Place two dinner plates in the oven to warm.

Spray two nonstick crêpe or omelet pans with nonstick vegetable spray. One pan should be about five inches in diameter. The size of the second pan is not important; it is merely used to finish the second side of the crêpes. Heat both pans over medium-low heat. Ladle about one-half cup of batter, or enough to coat the bottom, into the five-inch pan. Cook the crêpe until it is browned on the bottom, about a minute and a half. Lift the sides of the crêpe to be sure they are not sticking, then flip it out into the second heated pan and cook until browned on the second side. While the second side is cooking, ladle more batter into the first pan and repeat the process until you have made four crêpes. If you are not ready to serve the crêpes immediately, keep them warm, uncovered, in the preheated oven.

## MANGO-MINT SALSA

1 large tomato
1/2 ripe mango, peeled, seeded, and diced
1 small ripe avocado, peeled, seeded, and diced
2 tablespoons finely chopped fresh mint
1 tablespoon fresh lime juice
1/8 teaspoon salt

Peel the tomato by submerging it in a pot of boiling water for ten seconds. If you prefer a chunkier texture, you may leave the skin on the tomato. Dice the tomato. Combine all of the ingredients in a bowl, adjusting the salt and lime juice to taste.


## THREE-CITRUS SALAD WITH RASPBERRY PURÉE

1 large navel orange
1 Ruby Red grapefruit
1 tangerine
1/2 cup raspberries

Remove the citrus sections and raspberry purée from the refrigerator. Spoon a few tablespoons of the purée onto each of the two salad plates and rotate the plates to distribute the purée evenly. Arrange the citrus wedges like the spokes of a wheel, alternating the orange, grapefruit, and tangerine.

## SPICED CHAMOMILE TEA

To heat the teapot, fill it with boiling water. Let it stand for a few minutes, and then pour out the water. Drop in two chamomile tea bags and two whole cloves. If you have any fresh mint leaves left over from making the salsa, add a few leaves to the pot. Refill the pot with boiling water and let steep for at least five minutes.

## SERVING BREAKFAST AT THE SPA

Arrange two corn crêpes on each warmed dinner plate, laying them side by side, slightly overlapping. Spoon a tablespoon or two of salsa next to the crêpes, and serve the remaining salsa in a small bowl. Place a dinner plate and a salad plate of citrus on each tray. Set out your favorite tea service and a pitcher of ice water, refreshed with thinly sliced rounds of lemon.

Finally, slip into white terry-cloth robes and enjoy your delicious and guilt-free, luxury breakfast.

# First Light in Bangkok

*Griddled Coconut Rice Cakes*

*Siamese Spiced Papaya*

*Curried Breakfast Sausage*

*Thai Iced Coffee*

Breakfast Thai-style is a morning celebration of the complex
and seductive flavors of the East. Crisp coconut-milk flavored
rice cakes and sausages touched with a hint of curry contrast
delightfully with the mildly tart, vibrantly orange-spiced
papaya. Welcome to the Orient.

PREPARATION TIMES
*The Night Before — Forty Minutes*
*Wake Up Call — Fifteen Minutes*

## THE NIGHT BEFORE

*For the Coconut Rice Cakes:* Shake the can of coconut milk vigorously. Combine the coconut milk and water in a medium saucepan. Add the salt and stir with a wire whisk until smooth. Bring the liquid to a boil. Stir in the rice, turn the heat down to low, cover, and let simmer for about eighteen minutes. Be careful not to let the rice burn.

When the rice is cooked, transfer it to a mixing bowl. Beat the egg lightly with a fork in another bowl. Let the rice cool for ten minutes. Add the beaten egg while the rice is still warm and mix well, using a fork. Gather about one-half cup of rice in your hands and form it into a patty about one-half inch thick. Set it aside on a plate and repeat the process with the remaining rice to form six cakes in all. Cover the rice cakes and refrigerate.

*Prepare the Spiced Papaya:* Cover and refrigerate.

*For the Curried Breakfast Sausage:* Place four uncooked breakfast link sausages in a small sauté pan. Cover them halfway with water. Let them poach gently for ten minutes, turning them once. Remove the sausages and pat them dry. Sprinkle three-quarters teaspoon curry powder on a sheet of waxed paper. Roll the sausages in the curry powder to coat. Let them cool a bit, then cover and refrigerate.

*For the Thai Coffee:* Brew a pot of strong coffee. Let it cool, then transfer to a pitcher. Cover and refrigerate.

*Prepare the Breakfast Trays:* Line two breakfast trays with bamboo or woven straw place mats. Use batik-patterned napkins and place a spray of tiny orchids on each tray. Miniature carved elephants will add the charmed touch of Thailand. Provide soup spoons and chopsticks for Thai-style dining.

## GRIDDLED COCONUT RICE CAKES

One 14-ounce can unsweetened coconut milk
3/4 cup water
1/2 teaspoon salt
1 cup long-grain rice
1 large egg
Vegetable or peanut oil for frying

Remove the rice cakes from the refrigerator. Spread a thin layer of vegetable or peanut oil in a large nonstick frying pan. Heat the oil and fry the rice cakes over medium-low heat, turning once, until they are light golden brown on both sides. Drain on paper towels.

## SIAMESE SPICED PAPAYA

1/2 cup water
2 tablespoons sugar
3 tablespoons rice wine vinegar
1/2 stalk lemongrass, minced (optional)
1-inch cinnamon stick, broken in half
4 whole cloves
1/2 papaya, seeded, peeled, and cut into 1/2-inch chunks

Combine the water, sugar, and rice wine vinegar in a small saucepan. Place the lemongrass, cinnamon stick, and cloves on a four-inch square of cheesecloth, tie into a pouch with kitchen string, and add to the saucepan. Bring the liquid to a boil, reduce the heat, and let simmer gently for ten minutes. Remove the pot from the heat and drop in the papaya chunks. Let cool, then transfer the papaya and the liquid, with the cheesecloth bag of spices, to a bowl. Chill. Remove the spice bag before serving.

## CURRIED BREAKFAST SAUSAGE

Remove the sausages from the refrigerator. Lightly oil a small skillet with vegetable or peanut oil. Fry the sausages over medium-low heat until lightly browned on all sides, about ten minutes. Remove and drain on paper towels.

## THAI ICED COFFEE

Fill two tall glasses with cracked ice, then pour in the cold coffee. Add about one tablespoon sweetened condensed milk to each glass. Stir well to combine.

## SERVING BREAKFAST IN BANGKOK

Arrange the rice cakes to one side on simple white dinner plates. Remove the papaya from its liquid using a slotted spoon and arrange the fruit down the center of the plates, keeping it separate from the rice cakes so they stay dry. Garnish the papaya with sprigs of fresh mint. Place the sausage on the remaining third of each plate. Position the dinner plates on the trays along with the tall glasses of iced coffee.

Wrap yourselves up in cotton kimonos to add a touch of Oriental elegance to your meal. Burn a stick of sandalwood incense in the bedroom for just a few moments and the mood will be set for your exotic morning sojourn.

# Morocco at Dawn

*Marrakech Couscous with Scrambled Eggs*

*and Roasted Tomatoes and Peppers*

*Oranges and Dates in Orange Syrup*

*Tangier Mint Tea*

Begin an exotic morning with the marvelous seasonings and
textures of Moroccan food. The comforting flavors of eggs and
couscous come alive with the color and excitement of smoky
roasted tomatoes and peppers. A delightful compote of
oranges and dates completes this magic carpet adventure.

PREPARATION TIMES
*The Night Before — Forty Minutes*
*Wake Up Call — Fifteen Minutes*

## THE NIGHT BEFORE

*Prepare the Roasted Tomatoes and Peppers:*  Preheat the broiler or grill. Arrange the tomatoes and peppers on the broiler pan or grill and place them two to three inches from the heat. Broil or grill, turning them frequently, until they are charred and blistered on all sides. Wrap the peppers in a plastic bag and let them sit for ten minutes to loosen the skin. Meanwhile, slip off the tomato skins, cut the tomatoes in half, and squeeze out and discard the seeds and juice. Cut the peppers in half. Cut away the stems and cores. Peel off and discard the skins. Finely chop the tomatoes and peppers.

In a medium bowl, mix together the remaining ingredients. Add the chopped tomatoes and peppers, toss gently to combine, and adjust the seasonings. Cover and refrigerate.

*Prepare the Oranges and Dates:*  Cover and refrigerate.

*Prepare the Breakfast Trays:*  Place two small sprays of roses on individual brass serving trays. Set the trays with soup spoons, paisley napkins, and pieces of wheat lahvosh. The lahvosh is used to scoop the couscous onto the spoon.

# MARRAKECH COUSCOUS WITH SCRAMBLED EGGS AND ROASTED TOMATOES AND PEPPERS

## ROASTED TOMATOES AND PEPPERS

2 large ripe tomatoes
2 medium green bell peppers
1 1/2 tablespoons lemon juice
1 1/2 tablespoons olive oil
1/2 teaspoon cumin seeds
1 tablespoon minced fresh cilantro
1/4 teaspoon salt
Freshly ground black pepper

## MARRAKECH COUSCOUS

2/3 cup water
1/8 teaspoon salt
1 tablespoon butter
1/2 cup quick-cooking couscous

## SCRAMBLED EGGS

3 large eggs
Dash of salt and dash of freshly ground pepper
1 tablespoon butter
1 tablespoon sour cream

Take the Roasted Tomatoes and Peppers from the refrigerator and set aside.

Combine the water, salt, and butter in a saucepan and bring to a boil. Stir in the couscous. Cover the pan, remove from the heat, and let stand for five minutes while you prepare the eggs.

Break the eggs into a mixing bowl and beat them lightly with a fork. Season with the salt and pepper. Heat the butter in a nonstick skillet and add the eggs. Use a spatula or fork to stir the eggs, and let them cook until soft curds form. Remove from the heat and stir in the sour cream.

To assemble, pile a bed of couscous in the center of two warmed earthenware plates. Arrange the scrambled eggs in the middle of the couscous, and surround with a ring of roasted tomatoes and peppers.

## ORANGES AND DATES IN ORANGE SYRUP

2 large navel oranges
1/4 cup water
1 tablespoon honey
1/4 cup sugar
1 1/2 tablespoons Grand Marnier
2 tablespoons orange juice
3 fresh dates, pitted and minced

Wash and remove the peel from one of the oranges and cut it into very thin strips. Cut the strips into one-half-inch pieces. Put the peel in a small saucepan with water to cover. Bring to a boil and let simmer for ten minutes. Drain and rinse the peel in cold water, and drain on a paper towel.

Peel the second orange and cut the white pith and membrane from both oranges. Section the oranges, slicing between the membranes of each orange to remove clean segments. Work over a bowl to collect the juice.

Put the one-quarter cup water, the honey, and sugar in a small saucepan. Cook over medium heat, stirring until the sugar dissolves. Then bring to a boil over high heat and cook until a candy thermometer registers 230°F. Immediately remove from the heat and add the cooked peel. Let stand for fifteen minutes, then add the Grand Marnier and two tablespoons of the juice from the orange segments. Stir in the dates and orange segments. Chill.

## TANGIER MINT TEA

Bring three cups water to a rolling boil. Put one tablespoon green tea leaves, one-quarter cup sugar, and a handful of fresh spearmint leaves in a large teapot. Add the boiling water and let the tea steep for four minutes.

## SERVING BREAKFAST IN MOROCCO

Set the plates of couscous on the serving trays. Fill two ceramic soup bowls with the oranges and dates and add these to the trays. Serve the mint tea in tall heatproof glasses garnished with sprigs of fresh mint.

Cover your bed with an abundance of brightly patterned cushions for lounging the day away in your Moroccan oasis — and enhance your after-breakfast dreams with a stirring recording of "Scheherazade."

# SUNUP IN THE CARIBBEAN

*Jamaican Royal Fizz*

*Aruba Breakfast Plate: Islands of Eggs on*

*Lime-Scented Black Beans with Creole Coulis*

*Toasted Coconut-Orange Muffins*

Wake up to a Spice Islands breakfast, brimming with the
essential tastes of the tropics. Lime-infused black beans are
drizzled with zippy Creole Coulis and topped with perfect
poached eggs. After a few sips of your Jamaican Royal Fizz,
you will almost feel the warm tropical breezes.

PREPARATION TIMES
*The Night Before — Fifty-Five Minutes*
*Wake Up Call — Twenty Minutes*

## THE NIGHT BEFORE

*Prepare the Black Beans:* Cover the cooked beans, cool to room temperature, and refrigerate.

*Prepare the Creole Coulis:* Pour the coulis into a bowl, cover, and refrigerate.

*Prepare the Coconut-Orange Muffins:* Set the baked muffins aside at room temperature. Do not cover them.

*Prepare the Breakfast Trays:* Place a vibrant cloth of canary yellow, hot pink, or lime green on each breakfast tray. Heighten the mood with jump-up geometric-design napkins.

## JAMAICAN ROYAL FIZZ

In a blender, combine one cup orange juice, one-quarter cup light rum, one ounce Triple Sec or Cointreau, one egg white, two tablespoons heavy cream, one-quarter cup club soda, one-eighth teaspoon vanilla extract, and three ice cubes. Blend until smooth and frothy. Pour into tall frosty glasses, add straws, and garnish with spears of fresh pineapple. Serve at once.

## LIME-SCENTED BLACK BEANS

1 1/4 cups dried black beans, rinsed and picked over
1/2 onion, sliced
5 cups water
Salt to taste
1 lime, quartered and seeded

Place the beans, onion, and water in a medium saucepan. Bring to a simmer, cover, and cook gently for about fifty minutes, or until the beans are softened. Add salt to taste and remove from the heat. Very finely mince one lime quarter, including the peel. Add it to the beans. Wrap and refrigerate the remaining three lime quarters for garnish.

In the morning, reheat the beans. As they are heating, mash the beans gently with a potato masher, leaving some of them whole for texture. Adjust the salt, if necessary.

## CREOLE COULIS

1 tablespoon vegetable oil
1/2 onion, diced
1/2 green bell pepper, diced
1 stalk celery, diced
1 teaspoon paprika
2 large tomatoes, unpeeled and finely chopped

Hot pepper sauce to taste
Salt and freshly ground black pepper to taste

Heat the oil in a small sauté pan. Add the onion, bell pepper, and celery. Cook until the vegetables just begin to soften. Add the paprika, stir, and cook for thirty seconds. Add the tomatoes and their juice, and cook for three to five minutes, or until the tomatoes begin to soften and release more juice. Spice up the coulis with hot pepper sauce and salt and pepper.

In the morning, reheat the coulis before serving.

## ISLANDS OF EGGS

Fill a medium skillet with water and bring it to a boil. Reduce the heat to a simmer and lower two whole eggs into the water with a spoon. Count slowly to ten and remove the eggs from the water. Now, carefully break the eggs into the simmering water and cook just ten seconds. Then, using a slotted spoon, bring the whites up to cover the yolks. Adjust the heat so the water just quivers; it should not boil or the eggs will become tough. Cook the eggs for three minutes. Gently remove each egg with a slotted spoon, blotting the bottom of the spoon on a towel to remove excess water. Place an egg on top of each plate of beans and Creole sauce.

# TOASTED COCONUT-ORANGE MUFFINS

1 navel orange
1/2 cup (1 stick) unsalted butter, softened
1 large egg
1/2 cup fresh orange juice
1 1/2 cups all-purpose flour
1/2 cup sugar
1 teaspoon baking soda
1 teaspoon baking powder
3/4 teaspoon salt
1 cup shredded coconut, lightly toasted

Preheat the oven to 400°F. Using a zester or vegetable peeler, remove the zest from the orange and set aside. Remove and discard the pith from the orange, quarter the orange, and remove any seeds. Process the orange zest in the food processor until it is finely chopped. Add the orange, and process until coarsely chopped. Add the butter, and process to combine. Add the egg and orange juice and process to combine. Do not worry if the butter looks curdled at this point.

Sift together the flour, sugar, baking soda, baking powder, and salt into a large mixing bowl. Add the orange mixture and toasted coconut and stir to combine. Spoon the batter into lightly greased muffin cups, filling each one three-quarters full, making approximately fifteen muffins. (You may need to use two muffin tins.) Bake for twenty minutes, or until golden brown. Let the muffins cool on a rack. You may freeze the leftover muffins.

In the morning, loosely wrap four of the muffins in foil and reheat them in a 325°F. oven for eight to ten minutes.

### Serving Breakfast in the Caribbean

To assemble the Aruba Breakfast Plate, spoon a hill of black beans onto two colorful dinner-sized plates — Fiesta ware would be ideal. Top each mound of beans with half of the Creole Coulis and set a poached egg in the center. Garnish the plates with two of the reserved wedges of lime and sprigs of cilantro.

Position the plates on the trays, flanked by the tall cool glasses of Royal Fizz. Place the Toasted Coconut-Orange Muffins in a colorful napkin. Bring all four corners of the napkin together, tie it like a hobo's bag, and put it within easy reach.

Splash on some bay rum cologne, turn up the volume on your steel drum tape, and savor the flavors of the islands.

# MANHATTAN B AND B

*The* I'll Take Manhattan *Special:*

*Bagels, Smoked Salmon, and Cream Cheese*

*The Big Apple, Baked*

*Café Filtre*

The sophisticated atmosphere of a big-city morning-after is celebrated in this New York-style breakfast. Imagine the urban bustle outside your tranquil bedroom while you treat yourselves to bagels, smoked salmon, and the Sunday edition of *The New York Times.* Don't forget to unplug the phone!

PREPARATION TIMES
*The Night Before — Ten Minutes*
*Wake Up Call — Thirty-Five Minutes*

## The Night Before

*For the Special:* Slice the bagels and wrap them in aluminum foil to keep them fresh.

*For the Big Apple:* Using an apple corer or potato peeler, cut out the cores of the apples but leave the bottoms intact. Peel each apple halfway down from the top. The openings should be large enough to hold two to three tablespoons of filling. Rub the peeled surfaces with lemon juice, wrap the apples tightly in plastic wrap, and refrigerate.

Combine the raisins and Calvados in a small cup, cover, and set aside to macerate overnight.

*Prepare the Breakfast Trays:* Select place mats and napkins that sport a bold graphic black-and-white pattern. Use your most modern silverware and dishes. Slip a single white rose into an individual bud vase for each tray.

## THE *I'LL TAKE MANHATTAN* SPECIAL

2 bagels
1 small white onion
2 tablespoons capers
1 medium tomato, thinly sliced
1 avocado, peeled, seeded, and thinly sliced
3 ounces natural cream cheese
6 slices smoked salmon

Slice the onion paper thin. Place the slices in a bowl and add a few ice cubes, plus water to cover. Let the slices soak about twenty minutes in the ice water to remove their raw bite. Drain and pat dry with a towel.

While the onion is soaking, rinse the capers and pat dry. Slice the tomato very thin. Arrange the onion, capers, tomato, avocado, cream cheese, and salmon on a marble cheese tray or platter, fanning out the sliced ingredients.

Lightly toast the bagels. Place them in a basket lined with a white linen napkin to keep them warm.

## THE BIG APPLE, BAKED

2 pippin, Granny Smith, or other baking apples
Lemon juice
2 tablespoons raisins
2 tablespoons Calvados (apple brandy)
3 tablespoons granola
1 tablespoon honey, mixed with 1 tablespoon water
Heavy cream

Preheat the oven to 400°F. Unwrap the apples and stand them in individual ramekins. Mix the Calvados-soaked raisins with the granola and spoon the mixture into the apples, pressing it down. Baste each apple with a teaspoonful of the honey-water mixture. Bake for twenty-five to thirty minutes, depending on the size of the apples. Baste every ten minutes with the pan juices and the remaining honey mixture.

Before serving, spoon the pan juices over the apples. Accompany the baked apples with a small pitcher of heavy cream.

## CAFÉ FILTRE

You will need a French press coffeepot, one that is fitted with a plunger. Pour boiling water into the pot and let stand a few minutes to heat the pot. Pour out the water. For each six-ounce cup of coffee, add one coffee measure (one and one-half tablespoons) of medium-ground coffee to the pot. Fill with the appropriate amount of boiling water, stir, and let stand for three minutes. Gently press the plunger down to the bottom of the pot to trap the grounds underneath the plunger.

## SERVING BREAKFAST IN MANHATTAN

Arrange a steaming cup of café filtre and a dinner plate on each tray. Put a baked apple in its ramekin on each tray. Place the *I'll Take Manhattan* Special, warm bagels, pitcher of heavy cream, and a bowl of sugar on a table within easy reach of the bed.

Spread out the Sunday *New York Times*, tune the radio to the local jazz station, and settle in for what could be an all-day event.